Big Questions

By Richard A. Kauffman
Photos by D. Michael Hostetler

HERALD PRESS
Scottdale, Pennsylvania
Kitchener, Ontario

Scripture quotations, unless otherwise noted, are from the Revised Standard Version of the Bible, copyrighted 1946, 1952, © 1971, 1973.

BIG QUESTIONS
Copyright © 1982, 1984 by Herald Press, Scottdale, Pa. 15683
   Published simultaneously in Canada by Herald Press, Kitchener, Ont. N2G 4M5
International Standard Book Number: 0-8361-3353-6
Printed in the United States of America
Design by David Hiebert

84 85 86 87 88 10 9 8 7 6 5 4 3 2 1

Contents

Introduction

Does belief in God make sense? Why do some people have to suffer? Why am I tempted? Does God have a plan for my life? These are some of the big questions of life, questions which many thinking people have asked at some point in their lives. Artists, philosophers, and theologians have spent years—whole lifetimes—trying to answer them.

But what do they have to do with me? you might be asking. I have trouble enough figuring out who I am, not to mention who God is and whether he exists. Who am I? What can I make of my life? Do my friends really accept me? Why do my parents restrict me so much?

These are real questions too, BIG ones. But are they so different from the opening questions? For instance, whether or not you believe that God exists will make a great difference in how you answer the question of who you are. And if God does exist, is he a compassionate or a vengeful God?

Whether we begin with ourselves, or with God, or with the universe, it does not matter. But asking the big questions—the ones about the meaning of life—will force us to look beyond ourselves to God. We will try to look within ourselves from the viewpoint of God. Such a look can be a stretching, growing, even painful process.

This book, *Big Questions*, is designed to assist you in that process. It doesn't answer all the questions. In fact, sometimes you may think more questions are being raised than answered. But the book is written with the conviction that God created us with minds to think. God wants us to use them to think about the purpose of his

creation and our part in it, to probe into his revelation of himself in Christ and the Bible. We can share with others the insights we have into these questions and hear what others have to offer as well. Through this process it is our prayer that you will grow both mentally and spiritually, and that your understanding of God and commitment to him will be enhanced and deepened.

—Richard A. Kauffman

1. Does Belief in God Make Sense?

"Do I believe in God?" asks Woody Allen in his movie *Annie Hall.*

He answers his question:

"I did until mother's accident. She fell on some meat loaf, and it penetrated her spleen.... She lay in a coma for months....

"How can I believe in God when just last week I got my tongue caught in the roller of an electric typewriter? I am plagued by doubts. If only God would give me some clear sign! Like making a large deposit in my name in a Swiss bank account."

In his humerous manner, Allen expresses the doubts of many people.

Is it possible to still believe in God? How can we believe in God if plagued with so many doubts about his existence? How can we believe when there seem to be so few signs of his presence in our world? If we cannot believe in God, who or what can we believe in?

Are there any good reasons for believing in God? Or shouldn't we demand reasons? Should we be content to simply believe that he is?

Some people in modern times have said that God does not exist. Or we cannot know whether he exists; we simply must remain in doubt. Some have even said God died; he once was alive but now he's dead. Many people live as though God did not exist, even though they would claim to believe in God. But that is more of a distortion of belief than it is a well-thought-through case for unbelief, such as we wish to address here.

In fact, here in North America living as though God did not exist may be the most common unbelief. Numerous polls show that approximately 95 percent of the population holds to some kind of "belief" in God.

Occasionally, however, one is confronted with unbelief. How should one respond? We will explore this by first attempting to listen seriously to the critics of belief in God. Second, we will probe for fallacies in their arguments. Finally, we have to ponder some good reasons why believing in God does make sense.

Atheists (those who deny the existence of God) have their reasons for not believing in God, as well as theists (those who believe in God) have their reasons for believing in God. The atheists' arguments should not be taken lightly. We will note three of them, although more could be stated.

The Psychological Argument

First, there is the psychological argument. Belief in God, so it is said, is a childhood hangover, a pacifier of the mind. Adults who have not quite matured hang onto the notion that there is a kind being who loves them and cares for them just as they subconsciously remember being loved and cared for as an infant. For this position religion is mere fantasy, wishful thinking, wild imagining—an illusion, as the psychoanalyst Sigmund Freud, called it.

Now it is to the credit of these atheists that they've pointed out a characteristic of the faith of many people. Many God-believing people have not matured in their faith; they treat God like a big daddy in the sky who hands out spiritual lollipops when the chips are down.

But the other side of the argument is that religion is not a sign of immaturity for everyone, a sign of never having gotten rid of the blanket they clung to in childhood. For many, religion has been the life-changing force which has led to personal responsibility in the world and society, commitment to the needy and the downtrodden, and a giving up of personal ambitions and desires.

Consider, for example, a Mother Theresa in India who lives on almost nothing, and devotes all her waking time to ministering to the needs of the very poor and outcast people of the streets.

Religion may contain wishful thinking. But why not? Wishing and hoping are basic human expressions. We hope for a better world, we hope for a nice day, we hope for a good job. Why not hope that there is a benevolent and loving being who is our Creator and sustainer?

Some theologians have said that the mere hope in humankind that there is a God is a sign that God exists. However, we must point out that hoping there is a God does not prove that there is a God. But, on the other hand, asserting that there is no God does not prove that God doesn't exist.

Suppose that during a war a father disappeared. His wife is resigned to the idea that he was killed. But his son hopes, wishes, and dreams that he still has a father. The mother, prepared for the worst, says, "No, your father is dead." But the son persists in his dream that his father will someday return home.

Neither the son's dream that his father is still alive, nor the mother's resignation that he is dead proves anything about whether the father is dead or alive. He may, in fact, have been killed. Or he may have been taken prisoner of war and will be released after the war is over.

Wishing that God exists does not prove that he does exist. Nor does it prove he doesn't exist. In fact, it might be said that the psychological argument against God is wishful thinking too. What if God is a fearful, judging God? Then it would be better for ungodly people that he does not exist! Atheism may be merely wishful thinking.

The Social Argument

Next there is the social argument against the existence of God. According to this line of reasoning, religion is not so much a pacifier as it is a drug. "Religion is the opiate of the people," said Karl Marx. It is a way of dulling the senses of the poor and the oppressed so that they will not see their real state in life. Promise them pie in the sky, heavenly blessings, and they will be content with terrible conditions here in this life.

If the poor and the oppressed are to come to their senses, if they are to realize they are being kept down by the wealthy and powerful, then they will have to stop taking this strong drug, this opiate, religion. If they realize that all there is to life is this life, then they will rise up and revolt and throw off the strong arm of the rulers and the rich.

Again there is a partial truth in this argument. Religion has been used to keep down the poor and oppressed. Until the twentieth century there was an unholy alliance in many European countries between the state and the church. The state claimed absolute power over the people; and the church told the people that, since the state is ordained by God, they should obey the state. In return, the state supported—and controlled—the church. To some the church was seen as the enemy. Not only was the church discredited, but so was the object of its faith, God. God must go, many revolutionaries have said.

But on the other hand, there are also many cases of religion being a force for revolutionary change. In America the black church was active in ending slavery and in working in the civil rights movement. During the

Reformation, it was the simple faith of the Anabaptists which gave them the will to stand up against the power of both the church and the state in pressing for a believers' church—a church not under the control of the state.

Does this social argument prove that God does not exist? By no means. The abuse of religion by the powerful and the wealthy doesn't discredit faith in God any more than a few careless or unscrupulous doctors can discredit medicine. True, for too many Christians love of God has not resulted in love for the neighbor. Yet denying the existence of God does not necessarily lead to love of the neighbor.

The Scientific Argument

Finally, there is the empiricist, or sometimes called the scientific, argument against the existence of God. According to this line of reasoning, we cannot say that God exists because we cannot know him with our senses. We can't see, hear, smell, touch, or taste God; therefore God does not exist.

The empirical method of research used by the scientist means that we do not make any observations about the material world which are not based on observation with the five senses or cannot be measured with the use of scientific instruments.

The scientist cannot resort to belief in explaining the nature and function of the universe. He cannot say, "I believe this is the way it is." Or, "I hope this is the way it is." He must say that, based on the best empirical evidence available, "This is the way it is until we get further evidence." Many admirable gains have been made in using this approach. In the past too often the church has squelched the efforts of science. It is no wonder, then, that some scientists have reacted to belief in God. They cannot see God, they cannot measure God, and God has too often been portrayed by the church as an anti-scientific being.

For example, an Englishman who won a Nobel prize was asked, "Do you believe in God?" He indignantly replied, "No, I am a scientist." As if one can be a scientist or a Christian, but not a Christian and a scientist.

A completely honest Christian will have to admit that the universe is open to scientific exploration, and that given enough time, resources, and ability, many of its "mysteries" will be understood. But on the other hand, the honest scientist, whether theist or atheist, will have to admit the limitations of his own method. Science can only observe the inner workings of the material world. God is not matter; God is spirit. Therefore, the scientist as scientist will have to say he does not know whether God exists or not. He cannot prove, nor can he disprove, that God exists. As a Christian, of course, the scientist may want to affirm that God exists, but he will do so on other grounds.

What of the great questions of life: Why am I here? Where did I come from? What is the purpose of my life? What shall we do with the nuclear weaponry and the genetic engineering the scientists have given us? Can science claim to answer these questions? Pure science has no answers for them. We must look elsewhere for answers to the puzzle of the meaning of human existence.

Atheism

The three major arguments against the existence of God are troubling. They cannot be ignored. They contain partial truths. As one person has said, atheists are prophets who do only half the job; they cast down false idols, but they fail to replace the idols with the one, true God.

Because they fail to replace idols with the one true God, some atheists make a religion of atheism. Whether it be a belief in a utopian state (such as in communism), or in the inevitability of progress (Western democracy), or in the ability of science to solve all problems (scientism), they have an object of faith which they make into a god.

Atheists, though they have their reasons for not believing in God, have no proof that he doesn't exist. Neither do they have proof that the objects which they worship are worthy of such faith.

Finally, some atheists may secretly believe there is a God. But they may recognize that in believing in God there is a need for a change in life, a willingness to obey God's command. Unbelief, atheism if you will, is a convenient way of shutting the door to personal change and justifying a self-centered lifestyle.

A Case for God

Atheists have their reasons for not believing in God. Certainly, if faith is not to be irrational or merely wishful thinking, then believers too will have their reasons for believing in God.

Having reasons for believing in God is different, however, from being able to prove that God exists. If I say that a black cat is in the next room, we could go to the next room to observe whether or not this is true. If I claim that God exists, I cannot prove that God exists; there is not the same certainty in that assertion as in the mathematical equation $1 + 1 = 2$.

However, there are justifiable reasons for believing that God exists, and the case will be made that the reasons for believing in God are more convincing than the atheists' reasons for not believing in God.

Whence, whither, and why: these are the basic questions of life. Where do we come from? Where are we going? Why do we exist in the first place? In short, what is the meaning of life?

These are the questions with which philosophers have wrestled through the ages. These questions have haunted every thinking person in times of reflection, solitude, despair, and loneliness. These are the questions which every great religion, modern or ancient, has attempted to answer.

Have you ever ventured outdoors on a clear, starry night and been captured by the immensity, yes the limitlessness, of the universe? And then have you reflected on your own being, the fact that in the infinity of this limitless universe there is this finite being, this speck, you refer to as yourself? And then you wondered why?

Even in the modern era, after men have stepped on the moon, we continue to be haunted by the questions of our origin, destiny, and purpose. Maybe especially in modern times, when humankind is capable of destroying all life with nuclear weaponry, the questioning seems especially urgent.

One philosopher has summed up most succinctly these basic questions of human existence: "Why is there something and not nothing?" he asked. And the answer to that question is another question: Who has the better response to that question, the one who believes in God or the one who denies his existence?

Those who affirm the existence of God have an adequate answer to the basic questions of life. We can all agree, theist and atheist alike, that something exists. We are not only part of a cosmic dream. We have real minds, real bodies; that's a real world out there.

Only the theist can adequately answer the question as to where we have come from: we have come from God. We have not come from nothingness, we have come from something, that something which the Bible calls the Creator of the heavens and the earth.

A German scientist wrote a book called *In the Beginning, Hydrogen*. Hydrogen, he maintained, was the most basic element of all things. The question to put to that position is: Where did hydrogen come from? As a scientist he could not say. But as a believer one might say that all that is has come from God.

Clark H. Pinnock in *Reason Enough: A Case for the Christian Faith* says: Suppose that you took a trip from the United States to Canada. You passed the border and noticed a "sign" on a hill. It is a rock formation, spelling out the words: "Welcome to Canada." Would you assume that this intelligible rock formation was the result of rocks randomly rolling down the hill, ending up in this position quite by accident?

No, you would assume that some intelligent being gathered the rocks together and formed them in this way. Is it too much to believe that behind the intelligent designs of the universe there is an intelligent being? It is from this being that we have come.

Furthermore, the believer has an adequate answer to the question of where we are going, what our human destiny is. We cannot say that we're headed for nothingness, for oblivion. The believer asserts that just as God is at the beginning of our journey, he is also at the end.

Finally, theism most adequately answers the question of what our purpose is for being. If our origin is in God, if our destiny is toward God, then the purpose of our being is for God. In him we find the ultimate meaning. All other meanings we find in life are minor in comparison to this one.

If we give ourselves to a life of pleasure, it will pass. If we join a political movement, this too will pass. If we dedicate ourselves to a life of getting wealthy, what is the end of it? (No, you can't take it with you.)

Two theologians were once discussing the future of religion, how rapidly the world was changing, how remote the church sometimes was from the real world. Would the people continue to believe in God? they asked. One observed, "Just think of the people who are asleep beneath us in this building—what are the questions which preoccupy them? They are still the same questions which preoccupied [people] ... two thousand and more years ago: questions of guilt, suffering, love, justice in the world, the meaning of life and death."

There are no signs that these questions will soon die in the minds of humankind. And the answers are most adequately—and profoundly—to be discovered in God, the originator of all that ever was, is, and shall be.

But we repeat that believers cannot put forth proof for the existence of God, at least not proof that everyone will accept. But believers can put forth convincing reasons for the existence of God.

A Decision

Ultimately a decision must be made, for or against God. A decision must be made for ultimate purpose and meaning in life or the alternative: that life is a matter of chance, that there is no ultimate meaning, that one has to do the best one can to make something out of life.

The decision which is called for is trust, obedience, and belief: to accept meaning and purpose, to acknowledge by faith that behind and above and before all reality there is a supreme being into whose being we can entrust our own being, our whence, our whither, our why. And for Christians this being is best known through his Son Jesus Christ.

There is a story in Jewish literature in which a little boy with tears running down his face came to his father for sympathy. He tells his father that he had been playing hide-and-seek, but when he was in hiding no one would come looking for him. His father responds, "Perhaps you can better understand how the Almighty, who is hidden in mystery, feels when no one comes to seek."

On the contrary. God is no longer hidden in mystery. He has come to us in Jesus. Are we in hiding?

For Further Reading

Cassels, Louis, *The Reality of God.* Scottdale: Herald Press, 1972.

Küng, Hans, *Does God Exist?,* An Answer for Today. New York: Doubleday, 1980. Because the English translation of the above book was not available when I was writing, I used the Hans Küng lectures, "How Can We Talk About God Today?" given at the 1978 Fosdick Ecumenical Convocation on Preaching held at the Riverside Church in New York. This 839 page book is intended for very serious readers.

Phillips, J. B., *Your God Is Too Small.* New York: Macmillan Publishing Co., 1953.

Pinnock, Clark H., *Reason Enough: A Case for the Christian Faith.* Downers Grove: InterVarsity Press, 1980.

2. Do Miracles Happen?

It was a hot Saturday night in July—a great night for cruising, for being with friends, for living it up. By nine that evening I told my parents I was going to bed, supposedly to get a good night's rest. That was my cover (pun intended) for sneaking out to be with my friends.

The arrangements were made: at ten I would meet my friends—older than I and licensed to drive—at a corner near my house. The appointed hour came and I slipped into some clothes (new ones, mind you) and slipped out my bedroom window.

We had our fun that night, the three of us: cruising, dropping in on a friend who had a date, taking our frustrations out on some golf balls at a driving range. Then came the time for testing what my friend's new Chevy could do on the road.

The night was right, the car was in tip-top shape, with four brand-new tires and its convertible top down. We thought the night was right for testing our might. But the road we chose—the very one I lived on—was wrong. We should have known that you don't negotiate a steep hill, a curve, and a one-lane bridge which was designed for 35 miles per hour at the most at 80 miles per hour-plus speed.

The car sped through the bridge alright, but on the other side, now out of control, it hit a tree, head on. And then the lights went out, both mine and the car's. The only thing I recall was slipping in and out of an unconscious state the rest of the night. It was a kind of "sleep" that neither I nor my parents had anticipated earlier that evening.

I do remember being placed in an ambulance

alongside one of my friends. A nurse was there and I asked her, "Am I going to live?"

Her response was cautious, but the tone of her voice hopeful: "I don't know, but we'll do all we can to help save you."

Then, faced with the real prospect of death, I turned to my friend and said, "If God spares me, I'm going to give my life over completely to him." The lights went out again.

Of course, I woke up again and I lived to tell the story of a night out on the sly that ended with a bang. The lights came on, not just so that I could see with my physical eyes but so that I could see again, with my spiritual eyes, the presence and action of God in my life. To me, that was a miracle.

Why Miracle?

By its common definition a miracle is a happening which causes a sense of awe and wonder within those who observe it. It is something out of the ordinary, unique, foreign to common, everyday experience.

The word miracle has many meanings in our speech: "It was a miracle it didn't rain at our church picnic." "It was a miracle that Jim showed up on time for his dental appointment. He's usually late for everything!" "The varsity basketball team's league championship was miraculous. After all, they were the underdogs."

If everything is a miracle, then nothing is a miracle. Miracle, used too freely, loses its value and becomes meaningless. Why, then, should I take the liberty to describe the outcome of an auto accident as being a miracle? Because I believed then, as I do now, that God was acting in that event. Through it God spoke both a word of judgment and of grace.

Simply put, that is a miracle by the Bible's terms: an act of God in the course of history which brings either judgment or grace upon his people. The message behind the event is, "Repent, have faith; change your ways and follow me."

The accident for me was an act both of judgment and of grace. The previous year I had been running away from God, adopting a lifestyle far from Christian. God seemed very far away, so far, in fact, that in desperation I once prayed: "God, do something to bring me back to you." How he would answer that prayer I couldn't foresee.

There was also grace in that accident. Not only did God spare me, but he invited me back to him, to live a life of service to him, one filled with challenge and a sense of purpose. At times my response to him has been feeble, yet I do not doubt that he acted on my behalf to restore me to fellowship with himself and his people.

Some Popular Notions About Miracles

It has been assumed by many, Christian and non-Christian alike, that a miracle is a violation of the laws of nature. God, it is assumed, swoops down and invades the very world he's created, standing nature on its head: gravity suddenly yields to weightlessness; time stands still; matter disappears.

So far as I know, no physical laws were broken the night of my accident. We didn't rewrite the physical law that says no two objects can occupy the same space at the same time. The space occupied by the tree wouldn't give way to the car; and the space occupied by the car wouldn't give way to its passengers; so we were propelled out of the car and into a meadow.

Further, no medical history was written as a result of my injuries. Though I was severely lacerated from being thrown through a barb-wire fence—I still have the scars over a foot long on my stomach and legs—I received no fatal wounds from which I was spared by some supernatural power. The accident, as well as my recovery, have quite natural explanations.

The miracles in the Bible often involved nature. A storm was calmed or a person was healed. Sometimes the miracle involved a disruption of the laws of nature. How else can one explain the resurrection of Jesus, for example? That involved a total transformation of nature in quite a supernatural way. But a miracle need not necessarily involve a disruption of the laws of nature. The most important element in all the miracles in the Bible is not that they involved nature, but that they involved people. We might define miracle as an act of God in history, either of judgment or of grace, in which God calls a people to himself to live in fellowship with him and with each other. These "signs" or calls by God may be rather large or small events, but they are memorable.

C. S. Lewis in his book *Miracles* says that miracles are not in violation of natural law; they are rather the introduction of another factor (God's activity) into natural causation which produces a new result. As an example Lewis says that if you put six pennies into a drawer on Monday and six more on Tuesday, the law decrees that—other things being equal—you would find twelve pennies there on Wednesday. But if the drawer has been robbed, you may in fact find only two. What was broken was either the lock or the laws of England. The laws of arithmetic were not broken. The new situation illustrates the laws of arithmetic as well as the original situation.

Lewis concludes that a miracle is not an event without cause or without results. God caused the activity and its results follow according to natural law.

Two Interpretations

Lewis's story is adequate as far as it goes. However, it doesn't speak to a fundamental difficulty in the Christian's use of miracles. The skeptic can still raise the question of why, if a miracle has quite natural explanations, need we drag God into the picture? Why introduce this new element into the event when it doesn't seem justified on the basis of the event itself? For those of you who have had algebra, it would be like saying, if $a + b = c$, why throw x (God) into the equation: $a + b + x = c$?

Even in biblical times people had several interpretations of miracles. For instance, when Jesus healed the sick and cast out demons, some believed and some did not. Amazingly, we have no record that people didn't believe that Jesus did such works. But some believed that he did them because of the presence and power of God in their lives. And others "explained them away" by saying that it was because Jesus was possessed of demons that he was able to perform such deeds.

On the one hand, others responded with eyes of faith. They believed that God was demonstrating his power in and through the deeds of Jesus. The response to these deeds which Jesus desired was that of repentance and newness of life. That is the way of faith.

On the other hand, some would not or could not believe. Their eyes were closed. Sure, all could see the results of Jesus' actions; they were there in plain daylight for all to see. But some people refused to respond to God in Jesus, and found an escape route by saying Jesus' works were of the devil.

Today, as well, there are two interpretations of the activity of God in history, especially that activity which is recorded in the Bible. For the eyes of faith the forming of the people Israel, the coming of Jesus the Christ, his life, death, and resurrection, and the forming of the New Israel (the church) are all miraculous works of God. These works call for repentance, a new way of life, and participation in God's community, the church.

All of the action of God in history can be explained away by those who refuse to believe. Israel was merely a loose band of ethnically similar folk who found a common destiny by forming an alliance. Jesus was merely a reformer who tried to return his people to some former ideals. The resurrection merely took place in the minds of the disciples who were bereaving the loss of their loved one and leader.

The modern unbelieving mind, having no room for either the devil or God, will attribute the events of the people of Israel, Jesus, and the church to neither God nor the devil. They'll write them off by saying: look, there's a natural explanation for these events for which God and the devil are quite unnecessary.

In Bible times, as well as our own, the options still remain. On the one hand, the acts of God recorded in the Bible can be written off, explained away, or ignored. On the other hand, the eyes of faith will see in them divine purpose and meaning. They are acts of God calling people to repentance, faithfulness to him, and life in the community of believers.

Jesus—a Miracle Worker?

One of the greatest temptations facing Jesus was to be a sideshow artist in a circus of crowd-pleasing acts. He could have razzle-dazzled the people into the big tent of the kingdom of God, had he wanted to, with a marvelous, awe-inspiring bag of tricks. But he resisted the temptation to the end.

Jesus knew that for every person he could heal, every corpse he could bring back to life, and every disturbed mind he could straighten out, there would be thousands of lame, sick, and mentally deranged persons whom he could never reach before their death. Life is not all a matter of people being miraculously spared of that which ails them; Jesus knew the real world has its handicapped, premature deaths, and mentally unbalanced.

But the temptation was there. The devil tempted Jesus in this way (see the third temptation of Jesus in Luke 4:9-12), and the crowd pestered him for signs that he was in fact the Messiah (Luke 11:29, 30).

The devil and the crowd were testing Jesus, not at his

point of weakness, but at his point of strength. He was so fully convinced of his divine mission that he didn't have to prove he was somebody. He was so secure in being ordained of the Father that he didn't have to try to convince others by taking the role of a miracle worker.

For this reason, the Gospels seem to down play the miracles of Jesus. The Greek word for miracle (*thauma*) is not even once used in the Gospels. What the Gospels say is that some of Jesus' deeds induced in the observers a sense of awe and wonder. A form of the Greek word "miracle" is used to describe the effect Jesus' works had on others but not to describe the works themselves. Rather, the unusual acts of Jesus were referred to as "signs," "wonders," or "mighty works."

They were called "signs" because they didn't draw attention to themselves but pointed beyond themselves to the person and mission of Jesus. They were an announcement that in Jesus the kingdom of God was breaking out into the world and the power of the devil was being broken. The response that Jesus wanted to the work that he did was repentance, faithfulness, and a life of discipleship.

The people who were awestricken by the mighty deeds of Jesus were not necessarily the ones who followed Jesus to the end. In fact, the people who were amazed at the superhuman power of Jesus numbered among them some who believed that the source of this power was demonic rather than godly. Had they looked more closely at the results of Jesus' acts, they might have noted that they were deeds of mercy and benevolence (healing of sick, lame, and blind, for instance). Such acts are not usually attributed to the devil.

Truly, Jesus performed quite unique and unusual deeds. The greatest proof is that even his enemies recognized the power and authority in Jesus' works.

It is estimated that 20 percent of Jesus' activity had to do with healings. In addition, he cast out demons, raised

Lazarus from the dead, and had command over nature (the stilling of the storm, the withering of the unproductive fig tree). Jesus' life was characterized by miracles.

But remember, the Gospels call Jesus' acts "signs." And signs are not to call attention to themselves alone. They point beyond themselves. And we must get the point.

When Jesus healed people, the point is that God in Jesus was demonstrating his care and compassion for the sick. When Jesus cast out demons, the point is that God in Jesus was saying that the hold the devil has on the world is coming to an end. When Jesus commanded nature to obey him, the point is that God in Jesus is Lord over all, even nature.

The point of the signs and wonders is Jesus himself. He is the miracle, not just what he did, but who he was, the life and example he lived, what he taught, his death and resurrection. He was the main event.

In this Jesus we find both a window and a mirror. Through the window of Jesus we see God; God is revealed as a being of love and compassion. In the mirror of Jesus we see ourselves; we really are sinners and we ought to be faithful sons and daughters of God.

As Christians we can be expected to believe in the miracles of Jesus and of the Bible stories. But more is expected. What God expects of us is that we believe in the miracle himself, Jesus. Truly believing means that we have faith in Jesus, and that we obey his teachings, follow his example in all of life, and participate in the life of the community of faith (the church).

Do we get the point?

What About Me?

Some may say that I have taken some liberties in calling the auto accident I experienced at the age of fifteen a miracle. For miracles are either quite unique and unusual events or they are not miracles. Accidents from which people survive happen hundreds of times each day. Yet that event was life-changing and pointed me to God.

Because, as C. S. Lewis says, God doesn't shake miracles into the world like pepper out of a pepper shaker, we may be tempted to believe that they never happen. We may even begin to question whether the life of Jesus was really miraculous.

But the miracles of God in history have a long reach. We too can be a part of those miracles and their effect can reach out to us and transform us, if we will by faith and obedience respond to the *miracle* himself, Jesus. God is still working in the lives of people in both large and small ways. We too can be changed into new persons. And henceforth, life will never be the same for us. And that is a miracle.

For Further Reading

Lewis, C. S., *Miracles: A Preliminary Study*. New York: The Macmillan Publishing Company, 1947.

3. Why Is There Evil and Suffering?

Mary Jean was a most unusual girl. Few young people approach the kind of zeal for knowing and living the will of God as Mary Jean displayed in her life. She was so convinced of the need to seek God's will in her life, in fact, that for an extended period of time she went without food, slept on a hard surface, and rose early in the morning to spend several hours in prayer in search of God's will for her life.

When she became convinced that God was leading her to be a doctor, she threw herself into her studies. And though she studied hard enough to graduate from medical school with high honors, she still had time to devote several hours each morning to prayer and meditation before beginning her schoolwork. One of her schoolmates said of Mary Jean, "She was one of God's saints, walking this earth."

Only five days after graduation from medical school, Mary Jean was killed as a result of a tragic auto accident. Her parents and friends asked over and over again, Why? Why did this young woman who showed so much promise, who was so thoroughly dedicated to doing God's will, have to die so suddenly? Why did she who lived so fully have to die so early? Was it because of sin in her life?

Mary Jean's death seems a mystery. Like so many

who suffer and die, a sin—or any explanation—cannot be pinpointed. And still we ask, Why?

Who's to Blame?

Suffering, sickness, and death. How do you account for those who suffer innocently: the baby born with an enlarged heart, the teenager stricken with leukemia, six million Jews sent to the gas chamber by a madman called Hitler?

When we look to the Bible for answers to these questions, we'll discover there is some relationship between suffering and evil. Humankind must suffer because of the sin that entered the world with Adam and Eve. What we will also discover from the Bible is that it doesn't have one simple explanation or solution for evil and suffering. There are many. And no one response to suffering applies to every situation.

Some people, to be sure, can blame only themselves for their illness. If a young man is sexually promiscuous, he may have the consequences of his actions—in this case venereal disease. Suffering, however, is a much more complex human dilemma than to say it is the direct result of sin in every case.

In distress it is natural to look for answers to one's suffering or pain. For Christians, answers often fall into four categories: (1) we blame it on God, even though we may not say so in so many words; (2) we blame it on the devil; (3) we blame it on ourselves; or (4) we blame it on others.

What comfort is it when you've had an accident and are in pain to have someone say: "All things work together for good to them that love God"? The Apostle Paul had a profound idea in mind when he wrote those words (Romans 8:28, KJV). God does make good come out of bad, but many Christians twist the meaning of that verse to mean that God wills the bad that happens in life.

On the other hand, what kind of solution is it to blame your accident on Satan? Maybe you (or someone else) were simply careless. Why try to find a scapegoat in the devil? Someone might be at fault for the pain you are suffering, but it does nothing to explain the situation to blame it on the devil. Nor does it help you to cope with the pain.

Another response to suffering and pain is to blame it on oneself. At least, we wonder what we did to bring about the suffering. "Why is this happening to me? What did I do to deserve it? Is it because of sin in my life?" Soul searching at all times is healthy, but we cannot fasten blame too quickly—on ourselves or others. In the situation of pain and suffering, what God wills for us is to be released from guilt and to experience the comfort of his presence with us.

The sources of suffering and pain are many. Some suffering is the direct result of something I've done; other suffering I must endure due to someone else's wrongdoing; and some suffering has no good explanation.

Who's to blame if I get drunk, drive a car, and have an accident? Myself, of course. But suppose I am sober and driving a car carefully, observing all the traffic laws, and a drunk driver veers in front of me. Then who's to blame? Am I not innocent, even though I may have to suffer injury and pain?

Change the scenario again: what if, instead of a drunk driver coming into my path, it is a tornado that hits me? The tornado has a scientific explanation. But why should it hit the very place I am at the very same time I am there. Why me? Am I to blame? Is anyone else to blame? Does God will it? Did the devil put up this roadblock, hoping I would curse God and forsake him as a result? Does God control the tornado?

In trying to understand adversity and calamity, we humans often remain in the dark. Mystery surrounds suffering and death. We cannot explain it, though the depths of its meaning is at the heart of what it means to be human.

Asking the Right Questions

In the book *Night* Elie Wiesel, a Jewish writer who lived through a Nazi concentration camp during his youth, tells about a tragic incident in which another youth was hanged by the Nazis.

This youth was accused of being part of a plan to sabotage the camp by blowing up the electric power generating station. Whether he really was involved didn't matter to the Nazis. They were going to make a public example of this young man—all notions of justice and trial by jury were brushed aside.

And so the boy, along with two other adults in the camp, were dragged to the gallows. The several thousand Jews held in the camp were marched to the scene to witness it. Here was the ultimate threat: the Nazis were seemingly saying, "This is what will happen to you if you try to pull any tricks on us."

When the chairs were knocked out from under the three victims, the two adults died almost instantly. But the youth, because he was so light, experienced an agonizingly slow death while all the persons were forced to march by him.

Wiesel says that for more than half an hour the boy stayed there, struggling between life and death, dying in slow agony under their eyes. "We had to look him full in the face. He was still alive when I passed in front of him. His tongue was still red, his eyes not yet glazed."

Just as Wiesel was about to pass before the dying youth, a man called out from behind him, "Where is God now?" And Wiesel says he heard a voice within him answering: "Where is He? Here He is—He is hanging on this gallows. . . ."

What did Wiesel mean that God was hanging there on the gallows? Did he mean to say that God died? Or did he mean that God was there suffering with the dying boy? Whatever Wiesel meant, those two options are the most live options today for people who are troubled by the presence of suffering, injustice, evil, and death.

Some philosophers reason that an all-powerful, good God cannot coexist alongside of evil in the world. If God were good, he would want a perfect world. And if he were all-powerful, he would see to it that only goodness, beauty, and peace exist in his creation. But since there is evil in the world, then only one of three things have to be true: (1) God doesn't exist; (2) God exists, but he is either not a good or all-powerful God; or (3) evil, as the Christian Scientists say, is not real; it is an illusion.

The answer which some Christians have been able to accept for this philosophical dilemma is that of freedom. God created humans to be free, moral beings. Human beings are not robots hooked onto a divine computer responding in knee-jerk fashion to celestial signals beamed their way. Humans are free to be who they want to be. And to be truly free, they must know the difference between right and wrong and have the ability to choose between both options.

God could have created men and women who obeyed him without question. But how much greater it would be if God created people who, given the freedom to reject him, would actually love him instead. We are all like the son in the parable of the prodigal son. When we get to the end of our journey in search of freedom, we can return to the Father. God is there to welcome us home with open arms. There we find true freedom at last.

Back to Elie Wiesel. In the same book in which he tells about the hanging of a boy accused of sabotage, he tells how he faithfully said his prayers under the tutelage of a religious teacher. This teacher asked him one day, "Why do you pray?" And Wiesel didn't know how to answer. Why do you breathe? he thought to himself.

And then the wise teacher responded that true dialogue happens between God and a person when the person asks questions of God and God answers them. The mystery of prayer, said the teacher, is that God's answers are beyond our comprehension, and we won't be able to understand them until we die.

Then why do you pray? Wiesel demanded of his teacher. And he said simply, so that God will give me the right questions.

In looking to the Bible on the questions of evil and suffering in the world, we must be prepared to have our questions reshaped. Instead of asking how a good and all-powerful God can allow evil to exist in the world, the Bible asks another question, "How does a good and all-powerful God *confront* evil in the world? How is he *with* people who must suffer?"

To the question, Where is God when people suffer? the answer comes, God is in and with the sufferer. God took on flesh to suffer all that we humans must suffer, even death (Romans 8:31-39). He is with the young boy who seemingly is hung in innocence for an alleged crime in a camp run by criminals. He is with the young baby who is born with a partial lung and must gasp for every precious breath of a fleeting life. He is with the suffering of a young mother who is in the advanced stages of cancer and knows that in a matter of months she will have to say goodbye to her children for the last time.

It is one thing to say God is with us when we suffer for no wrong we've done, but is God with us when we suffer because of our own sin? Is God party to the sin? No, he is not with us in our sin, but he gives us that freedom to sin. Yet, to convince us that he really wants us to be faithful sons and daughters of his, he takes our sins upon himself in the cross of Christ, and woos us back to himself. And if we suffer because of our sins, God is there with us in our suffering. That is the message of the cross: God in Christ suffers with us because of our sins!

Does God Cause Evil?

Does God cause evil so that he can make it right? Did God deliberately cause the man to be blind (John 9) so that Jesus could heal him for the glorification of God? Some Christians think so. I disagree.

The very day on which I began to write this chapter on evil and suffering I twisted my back and strained it. This was actually a recurrence of back problems I had about three years before. Since that time I have been doing exercises to strengthen my back. They've helped a great deal.

Then with just a small turn of the back I felt that same snap in the lower part of the back. And the pain which follows. Why does it have to happen to me now? I thought. After all, I have to concentrate on this writing assignment. I haven't the time to go to the doctor or to be distracted by pain while writing.

Then it struck me that maybe the pain was meant to be. How appropriate that on the very day when I must write about suffering, I should be in pain. I won't write about the subject at arm's length; I'll write from personal experience.

"Praise God anyhow," some Christians would say. That part I can accept. But to blame God for the pain and suffering we humans must face is another matter.

Yes, good can come out of bad. The cross is the best example of that. But the cross was still the most evil, horrendous event in the history of the world. Good came out of evil; Christ was resurrected and through his death and resurrection we can be freed from sin and experience new life. But why call the *bad* of the cross good? Bad is bad, and good is good. Christ still had to agonize over whether he would allow himself to be crucified; he still had to suffer the pain of being on the cross and being forsaken by his Father.

Admittedly, the pain in my back is quite minor in comparison to the pain of Christ on the cross. But I'll still refuse to call it good, though some good things may come out of it.

When we are in pain we don't need to grit our teeth and say, "Thank God, anyhow." We can do what the people of the Old Testament did. They cried out in their pain, asking God for deliverance from it. Their prayers, called laments, didn't gloss over their desperate situation. They confronted it head on—and confronted God with it too.

> O Lord, how long shall I cry for help,
>   and thou wilt not hear?
> Or cry to thee, "Violence!"
>   and thou wilt not save? (Habakkuk 1:2)

Sometimes they even seemed to blame God for the problems which were brought upon them.

> Rouse thyself! Why sleepest thou, O Lord?
> Awake! Do not cast us off for ever! (Psalm 44:23, 24)

At least they blamed God for allowing worse things to happen to them than what happens to the sinful people who don't believe in him.

> Thou who art of purer eyes than to behold evil
>   and canst not look on wrong,
> why dost thou look on faithless men
>   and act silent when the wicked swallows up
>   the man more righteous than he? (Habakkuk 1:13)

Something amazing happens when the people of God complain to him about their problems. They confront the negative in their experience; and then, having unloaded their sorrows, they begin to see the positive side and end up praising God. It's not that their situation has changed; things may still be crumbling all around them. But their faith in God is renewed.

> Though the fig tree do not blossom,
>   nor fruit be on the vines,
> the produce of the olive fail
>   and the fields yield no food,
> the flock be cut off from the fold
>   and there be no herd in the stalls,
> yet will I rejoice in the Lord,
>   I will joy in the God of my salvation.
> God, the Lord, is my strength;
>   he makes my feet like hinds' feet,
>   he makes me tread upon high places
>   (Habakkuk 3:17-19)

The load is lifted again; I can step lightly!

Praise God anyway? Yes, but there is no shortcut to the praise of God. There's no escape from facing up to our suffering. But whether God relieves us of our suffering, or we must live with it awhile longer, God is with us, especially in our sorrow.

How foreign are these words in Coleridge's *The Rime of the Ancient Mariner* to one who senses the presence of God in his life during times of crisis.

> Alone, alone, all, all alone;
> Alone on a wide, wide sea,
> And never a saint took pity on
> my soul in agony.

Alone in agony? No, for God's comfort is near at hand. God's people are also available as servants of comfort, compassion, and assurance. We are not alone, for the church is a vital support to us when we suffer. Christians can stand with each other and, in a real sense, become a part of God's presence.

It was one of the distinctive emphases of the Anabaptists to see in the cross of Christ an example of the way Christians should live. God confronted the evil and suffering in the world by taking it upon himself through his Son Jesus. Likewise, those who call themselves Christians should take upon themselves a cross.

Where there is hate and hostility, Christian community absorbs the hate, works toward reconciliation, and refuses to fight back.

Where there is suffering, the Christian community reaches out in acts of mercy, tending to the needs of those who are of ill health, maimed, disabled, or mentally ill.

Where there is oppression and injustice, the Christian community binds up the wounds of those who are oppressed and tries to stand in the way of the oppressor, helping him to see that the oppressed is his brother.

This is the way of the cross. This is the way Christ lived—and died. It is God's way with his sinful, suffering, sorrow-filled people. It is the way to which we are all called.

For Further Reading

Hong, Edna, *If God Is Love: A Christian's Journey Through Suffering.* Minneapolis: Augsburg Publishing House, 1978.

Nisly, Paul, *Why Suffering?* Scottdale: Herald, 1980.

Simundson, Daniel J., *Faith Under Fire: Biblical Interpretations of Suffering.* Minneapolis: Augsburg Publishing House, 1980.

Wiesel, Elie, *Night.* New York: Avon Books, 1958, 1969.

Yoder, Jonathan G., *Healing: Prayer or Pills?* Scottdale: Herald Press, 1975. The story of Mary Jean at the first part of this chapter comes from this booklet, pages 52, 53.

4. Does God Have a Plan for My Life?

A story is told about a young man who was concerned to discover the will of God for his life each day. He developed a method in which each morning, as he arose from bed, he randomly flipped open his Bible to a page, put his finger down, and wherever it landed, he considered that verse God's will for him that day.

One morning, as he was doing this, he landed on the Scripture passage in which it tells how Judas went into the field to hang himself after betraying Jesus. Thinking to himself that this cannot contain any clues of God's will for that day, the young man flipped his Bible to another passage. And there it read, "Go and do thou likewise."

The question of what God wills for our lives is a difficult one. Does God have a plan for my life? If he does, is it my duty to find out what that plan is and then carry it out?

What is God's will for my life? Does he have a "plan" for me? If so, just how do I discover what that plan is?

It would be nice if God were to give us a call each day, filling us in on what he has in mind for that day. But God doesn't seem to use the Bell System.

The Christian life would be easier if God had a blue-

print for our lives, or a road map, or a guide of some kind, to let us know what decisions are ahead of us and how we would respond.

Now all of these ideas again raise the question of freedom of choice. Is our future predetermined by God? Do we have any choice in the matter? Or does God simply know ahead of time how we will live, but refrains from forcing any decisions on us?

If we don't have any choice about the future, then we don't need to worry about God's will. Whatever will happen will happen. It was predetermined by God; we had no choice in the matter.

The question of whether we have any freedom of choice in life is a knotty one for Christians. On the one hand, we believe that God is the Lord of the universe and of history. He is in control of the outcome of history.

On the other hand, must we say that God is responsible for what we do? That would mean that God is not just the originator of good but also of evil. Then we are not really responsible for our actions, God is. And if that were the case, why would Christ have had to die for the sins of the world? They were God's sins for which he died, not ours.

The Anabaptists affirmed three things about the freedom of the will. First, they said God is righteous; therefore he cannot be held responsible for evil. We are responsible for the evil deeds we commit; evil is the result of the freedom we have been given to love and obey God or reject him and be our own god.

Second, an indispensable experience for persons who wish to become Christians is that they repent of their past lives of sin and make a change. That demands freedom—the ability to turn one's back on a former way of life and choose a new way of life.

Finally, the Anabaptists maintained that the Christian way of life is a life of discipleship. To be a Christian is to follow Christ daily in the choices we make. To follow Christ means that we have exercised our freedom to be obedient to his teachings, rather than using our freedom to live as the world lives.

From a biblical viewpoint it is necessary to maintain that we humans have freedom of choice in life. To be truly human is to be truly free. To be truly Christian is also to be truly free. Although Christians are free to make completely individual choices, they choose to use this freedom to love and serve God instead.

So there must be genuine freedom of choice for the Christians in shaping their future.

A Process of Discovering

If I seem to be trying to destroy the idea that God has a plan for our lives, this should not be taken to mean that God doesn't will anything for our lives. God does will some things for our lives. We'll note at least three.

First, there may be several ways to be faithful to God's call for our lives. There is no *one* plan for us. Many options are open for us in life, some of which would be better for us than others from the divine perspective, but usually there are numerous ways we can be faithful to God's call in our lives.

Two friends of mine hold two views of marriage. Sue believes that there is only one person right for her to marry. She is hoping to meet that person and when she does, she wants him to be her husband. Don believes that there probably are a number of women in the world with whom he could be compatibly married for a lifetime.

Here I side with Don. Several options are frequently open to us which would fall under God's will.

Second, the matter of God's will being done in our lives has to do with a lifelong process of discovery. It's not a matter of now you have it, now you don't. All through life we must be in search of God's best for us.

The certainty with which we believe God's will is being done in our lives is not a good indicator of whether in fact it is being done. Some people do most unchristian and unethical actions and say that God is working out his will in their lives. Some people defended the Vietnam War, for instance, on the grounds that it was God's will that South Vietnam be maintained as a country which was open to Christian missionaries even if war was necessary to keep it open. The gospel was being spread by the use of the sword, in other words. How foreign that is to the will of God and the gospel of peace which Jesus taught.

In this process of discovering God's will, we would do well to always be somewhat skeptical about our own choices. The mind plays tricks on us. What we consider sometimes to be God's will might be merely our own will which we hope God will endorse.

Third, in the process of discovering God's will we are co-creators with God of our own destiny here in this world. The Apostle Paul says we are to "work out our own salvation with fear and trembling; for God is at work in you, both to will and to work his good pleasure" (Philippians 2:12, 13).

These words may sound strange in coming from the apostle who said that we cannot earn our salvation, that no good works, only the grace of God through faith in Jesus Christ, can save us. But Paul has not changed his mind about the way we are saved. Rather he is saying that the way this "saved life" works itself out in our experience is largely up to us. The "fear and trembling" is the humility with which we believe that God's will is being done in our lives.

Yet, at the same time, this process of discovering the will of God and of being co-creators and co-partners with God in shaping our lives can be a joyous experience. We can be confident that God's will will be done, that he is with us, even if and when we make mistakes.

Preoccupation with the idea of finding God's will for

our lives can be a sign of not wanting to take on our God-given responsibility to work out our own salvation. Perhaps we don't want to risk making decisions for fear of making the wrong ones and failing.

A friend of mine who grew up on a farm said that when he was a boy his father had to tell him each time what chores he was to do. But as he got older he knew himself what needed to be done and what was expected. His father didn't have to tell him, nor did he need to run to his father and ask him.

My friend says that this is the way he's experienced the Christian life. As a young Christian he was not sure of himself as to what God wanted him to do. But as he matured, it became clearer to him in the decisions he faced in life what was expected of him by God. He no longer needed to reflect so much on what he should do. He needed to act on what he believed to be the right course of action.

Guidelines for the Discovery Process

God doesn't call us up every day, courtesy of Ma Bell, to fill us in on that day's plans. Nor does he drop a blueprint out of the sky to inform us on how our life is to take shape. But we are not without guidelines as to how to live and what choices are appropriate for us to make. We will suggest two of these: seek first the kingdom of God and discern and use your gifts.

Seek First His Kingdom

Oftentimes when we are thinking about God's will for our lives it is in the context of making vocational decisions. What am I to do with my life so far as a job is concerned? How should I earn a living?

Those concerns, though important to God because he is so thoroughly concerned about us, are not his primary concern. God's primary interest is that we should seek "first his kingdom and all these shall be added to you as well" (Matthew 6:33).

Two aspects of this verse need clarification. First, the "other things," what are they? The context of this verse is how I'm going to earn a living, that is, put food on the table, clothes on my back, and a shelter over my head. In other words, what kind of job should I engage in for life?

Jesus said: Don't be so concerned about those details of life. They will work themselves out. After all, note how God takes care of the birds of the air and the lilies of the field. God will take care of us. If we really seek first his kingdom, it will become obvious to us how to earn a living—what job to engage in, in other words.

What does it mean, then, that God's primary will for us is to seek his kingdom? What is God's kingdom? The kingdom of God is often defined as the rule of God in the lives of his people. But to say that we are to seek God's rule in our lives is no more concrete or helpful than to say, Seek his will in your life.

Perhaps it helps to say that God's kingdom is being established wherever and whenever reconciliation takes place. It happens between God and people; and it happens between people on earth. Paul said that Christ reconciled us to God. Now we are to be reconcilers bringing people together with God and people with people (2 Corinthians 5:18, 19). It means establishing peace, fellowship, and harmony where there was once hatred, fighting, war, and alienation.

If you want to know whether you are in God's will, ask yourself whether what you are doing is building God's kingdom—bringing people together and to God—or whether it is serving some other purpose—such as meeting your own selfish needs.

Discern and Use Your Gifts

One of the parables Jesus told was about a master who, when he went on a journey, left his assets to the stewardship of three servants (Matthew 25:14-30). To one he gave five talents, another two, and the third one.

When the master returned from his trip he inquired of his servants what they had done with their talents. The first servant had invested the five talents entrusted to him and had earned five more talents. That pleased the master. Likewise, the second servant had used his two talents wisely and had gained two more talents. Again the master was pleased.

When it came time for the accounting of the servant who was given one talent, he came forward, hung his head, and said, "I was afraid I might lose what you had given me, master, so I went and buried it in the ground."

The master was furious. He took the one talent from that servant and handed it over to the one who had ten talents.

I used to feel sorry for the fellow who was punished for having only one talent. It seemed unfair to give him only one talent and then punish him on top of that. Why did the master punish the third servant for having only one talent when he was the one who had given him only one talent in the first place?

This misses the whole point of the parable. What matters to God is not how many talents and personal gifts we have, whether it's ten, five, or one. What matters is what we do with the talents we do have.

We often think that we're not talented. Perhaps that is due to a too limited view of what talents are. Often in school it is the ones who have artistic or athletic ability who are labeled talented.

But it is a gift to be able to relate to people, or to think clearly about issues facing the world, or to see beauty where others see only the ordinary, or to take time to be with others in a relaxed manner, or to fix an ailing automobile.

When we compare ourselves to others, and feel we aren't nearly so talented as they, we end up spinning our wheels and neglecting to use the talents that we do possess.

God will not ask us to do that for which we don't have the necessary skills. If you are not musically inclined and don't have nimble fingers, he's not going to call you to be a church organist.

What God calls us to do we should enjoy doing because it is a part of our nature and we can do it well. This is contrary to the popular notion that God's will is always contrary to our own will.

A woman who was a candidate for the mission field told her mission board, "I'll do anything you ask me to do as long as you don't ask me to teach." The mission board was curious as to why she didn't want to teach.

"Because I enjoy teaching so much!" was her answer. She seemed to think that doing God's will meant doing something she surely wouldn't enjoy.

Sometimes we are called upon to do things for which we feel we have no gifts. Perhaps it's a matter of God being able to use us best in areas where we feel we are weakest and sense the need to rely totally on his guidance and strength. Or it might be a case of uncovering talents that we didn't even know we had.

We discover our talents through trying them, either through education, part-time jobs, volunteer work, hobbies, or work in the church. As long as we approach each new activity, job, or course with a spirit of adventure, of trying it out to see whether we like it and are good at it, we need not be fearful of failure.

A Jewish man named Zusya went to his rabbi and asked, "How can I live so that I might be as great as Moses?" And the rabbi responded, "When you get to heaven, God won't ask you why you weren't Moses, he'll ask you why you weren't Zusya."

Each one of us is entrusted with a unique complex of likes and dislikes, gifts and abilities. It is our Christian duty to discover them and use them for the good of God's kingdom, not for our own selfish gain.

The Church Can Help

The role of the church in helping its members discover and use their gifts has been changing during the last number of years. Many Christians now believe that one of the primary functions of the church is to discover with its members what their gifts are and how they can best put them to use.

This has been my happy experience. In college I was a music major, but by the time I graduated, a profession in music did not seem to satisfy some of the aspirations I had. From there I went to seminary, pastored briefly, and then became a conference youth worker.

It was while I was in this last position that the conference decided to initiate a monthly newspaper. They asked me whether I'd be interested in being its editor. What they didn't know was that I had a great deal of interest in editing, though they must have sensed some gifts in this direction.

After several years as a youth worker and news editor, the editorship of *With* magazine, the youth publication of several Mennonite denominations, became available. Someone thought to himself, "Richard Kauffman is a youth worker and an editor; maybe he could be the editor of a youth magazine." So I was asked to take the job.

That is how I got my present job. Looking back I can see the hand of God and the affirmation and discernment of people in the church, helping me discover God's will for my life.

Sometimes we need to seek out that discernment or counsel. Perhaps we need to go to a pastor or a parent or a mature Christian we respect. Or the counsel might come through a group—a small group, a youth group, or a Sunday school class.

We can delude ourselves into thinking we are gifted in an area in which we really are not. Or we may think it is God's will we are choosing when we are really choosing an option for our own selfish reasons. A group can see us in a way we cannot. Other people's questions, suggestions, and advice should help us to consider alternatives and issues we could not have thought of ourselves.

In a group there are the resources of prayer and group study of the Scriptures. The group can pray with us, support us, affirm us, and keep a check on how the process of discovering God's will is working out in our lives. And if we experience failure, the group should be there to pick us up and get us going again.

An Assuring Word

Sometimes we are tempted to want to know the will of God so that we can then choose whether or not to live by it. We are also tempted to know what we plan to do and then seek God's blessing for it. I know these temptations because I have yielded to them both.

The so-called problem of God's will is not so much a matter of the mind (knowledge) as it is of the will. If we are truly willing to do God's will, and then we seek it, we will find it. That is a promise.

For Further Reading

O'Connor, Elizabeth, *Eighth Day of Creation: Gifts and Creativity.* Waco, Texas: Word Books, 1971.

Vogt, Virgil, *The Christian Calling.* Scottdale: Herald Press, 1961.

5. Why Am I Tempted?

When I was just entering the teen years I was deeply troubled by new urges I felt. Specifically, I was increasingly aroused sexually, especially at the sight of beautiful women and girls. As hard as I tried not to succumb to this desire, so much harder was I tormented by a sense of being a lost and godforsaken person, on his way to hell.

Maybe it was an overactive conscience that was at work in my case. Certainly I took the Bible seriously when it says that a man commits adultery with a woman just by looking lustfully at her! If only I could have gouged out my right eye or cut off my right hand. But then there's always the other eye and the other hand to contend with!

Frustration gave way to courage one day, courage to talk to an older, mature Christian. Or was it in desperation that I opened up myself? Slowly I led him into the subject. It's better to lead someone cautiously into the pits of your darkened, inner self; that way the other person can adjust to the dimmer light as you stumble step-by-step into that cavernous cellar. He may not even notice the lessening of candlepower.

As I opened myself up, the darkness actually began to lift. Some lights went on, not only for me, but for the other person. Can you believe that this older, more mature Christian, actually saw in me something of himself?

"You know," he said, "I have the same struggles too. I think I know something of what you're going through."

Those weren't his exact words, but he said something to that effect. He didn't condemn me, as I had expected. He didn't immediately prescribe anything—like more daily Bible reading and prayer. He listened and then let it be known that the kind of temptations I faced were not just my own; others faced them too. And that God knows our hearts and if we really want to do what is right, he'll help us to do it.

Not alone in our temptations. Not alone! Every temptation to sin which ever throws its enticing lure in front of us has been faced by someone else. To be human is to be tempted.

It's Tempting

If, as an early teen, I had an overactive conscience, later in life I went through a stage in which I tried to domesticate it—retrain it so that it would feed back to me what I wanted to hear.

For instance, take the issue of lust; for awhile I reasoned with myself. Look, I am a full-blooded male of the human race. That means I have certain desires and appetites, sex being one of them. That's the way God made me. It is natural for me, as well as most males, to like the looks of a beautiful woman. It is even natural to have evil thoughts and desires about them. Can I help it if that's the way I'm made? The result of this was that for a time I gave in to the temptation to look lustfully at women—all on the basis of some reasoning I had done in my head.

When Evil Seems Good

My experience leads me to note three things about temptation. The first is that temptation often has a way of presenting itself to us in such a way as to make evil seem good, or the wrong thing right. Our mind can do intellectual somersaults and we can end up standing what is morally right upside down. Then our mental somersaults make what is really wrong seem right; and what is really right seem undesirable.

For instance, the biblical view on sex is that it is a good and natural part of God's creation, but that sexual intercourse belongs in marriage when a couple loves each other and has a lifelong covenant to be faithful to each other.

Today we hear all kinds of "good" reasons why this biblical standard for sexual conduct need not be maintained:

• The average age for marriage is going up. At the same time the age of puberty is going down. If youth are sexually capable and marriage is postponed till later in life, should it not be okay for them to be sexually active if they take precautions not to conceive any children?

• One of the reasons for a biblical prohibition against sex outside of marriage was to protect the family and to avoid the birth of unwanted children. But the Bible was written before the era of reliable birth control.

• If sex is the highest experience of love, and a couple really loves each other and are committed to one another, shouldn't sexual intercourse be an acceptable form of the expression of their love for each other?

• Trying out sex before marriage is a good way for a couple to test their sexual compatibility. A couple should have the assurance before entering into marriage that they are sexually compatible.

• Everyone's doing it. The person who enters into marriage as a virgin is being cast as the oddball, the one who has not quite gotten with the modern, more advanced and superior attitudes toward sexual morality and practice.

Aren't these all good-sounding arguments why the biblical standard of sexual morality need not be taken seriously? Yes, and the approach is not new. Jesus warned about false prophets who would come dressed like sheep but in reality they are hungry wolves (Matthew 7:15). What they have to say will sound very innocent, perhaps even pious. But in reality their aim is to deceive you and lead you away from what God wills for your life.

When Temptation Questions God

Which leads to the second point about temptation. Not only does it trick us into thinking that something bad is really good; it takes us further in the direction of questioning God. The question floating around the Garden of Eden before humans sinned was, Did God really say ...? Did he really tell us that we weren't to eat of the tree of the knowledge of good and evil? Maybe we heard him wrong. Or maybe he didn't really mean what he said (Genesis 3:1-7).

In my case, I was tempted to say that Jesus couldn't have meant literally what he said in Matthew 5:28: "Every one who looks at a woman lustfully has already committed adultery with her in his heart." Obviously, Jesus was engaging in overstatement here. He wasn't saying that lust is in reality the same thing as adultery. What he was saying was that lust is what leads to adultery and that one must be careful not to give in to one's lustful desires because the end of that is adultery. See how easily we twist what God does say.

Who Is Our God?

The third characteristic of temptation is really the most central one. What is at stake when we are tempted is, "Who will be our god? Who will be in charge of my life? Will it be God himself, our Creator? Or will it be ourselves and our own selfish and sinful desires?"

When we talk about sin we usually have in mind certain practices, such as killing, cheating, stealing, lying, and so forth. But fundamentally, sin is trying to be our own god, trying to be *like* God, in fact (see Genesis 3:5). These other individual sins are expressions of this one, basic sin of setting ourselves up as the lord of our own lives.

Passing the Buck

Even though at heart we are the ones to blame for yielding to temptation, the human tendency is to find a scapegoat. We want someone else to blame.

Some people try to blame their sin on God. He made the world this way, after all. If he didn't want us to sin, why does he allow sin? But God cannot be blamed for sin, for he is a righteous God who causes no one to sin (James 1:3).

Some people try to blame others for their sin. Adam was the first master of the art of passing the buck. He tried to lay his own guilt on Eve. We often think it really wasn't my fault that I did such and such. If I hadn't happened to be with the group when it happened, I would not have ever been implicated in the deed. We pass off our guilt to group pressure, enticing advertising, or being trapped by a wily person.

Others, of course, blame Satan. He's the one to blame for temptation to sin, therefore, he must assume responsibility for my having given in to sin.

The power of Satan in the world must be reckoned with: Jesus had to wrestle with it, Paul struggled with it, and every Christian since knows from experience the persuasive powers of evil in the world. But because Christ overcame sin, we too can. So there's no excuse when we give in to temptation; not even Satan can be used as our scapegoat.

We humans must assume responsibility for our sin. We can't pass the buck, not to God, not to others, not even to Satan. We alone must accept the guilt. "Each person is tempted when he is lured and enticed by his

own desire" (James 1:14).

Will I try to be like God by being lord over my life? Or will I allow God to be my lord, live in his image, and reflect his attributes of love, truth, and righteousness? These questions are the fundamental issues at stake in the matter of temptation.

Coping with Temptation

There is probably no more graphic portrayal of the struggle with temptations by persons who want to do right than that of Paul's in Romans 7. He speaks for all Christians when he says that what he wants to do, he does not; and what he doesn't want to do, he does. Read about his struggle and see if you can identify with it.

What Paul refers to is sometimes called the sins of omission (failing to do what we ought to do) and commission (doing what we ought not do).

However we classify right and wrong, all of us get caught between the two. Where can we find the strength to do what is right and to avoid what is evil? How can we cope with temptation? Even more, how can we be victorious over it?

We are not alone in our temptations ... remember that thought. Roll it around in your mind. Jesus is with us in our temptations. He's even experienced everything that we have ever experienced in the way of temptation. So we need not feel lonely in confronting temptations.

Speaking of being alone in temptation! Jesus was alone in the desert. There he had to face the temptations of Satan head on.

If we think that the temptation to become wealthy or at least to assure ourselves that we can live comfortably is especially alluring in our society, look at Jesus' experience (Matthew 4:3-4). This was the temptation Satan first put to Jesus, to turn stones into bread. Then Jesus would have no worries about having plenty of food; he could even look out for the needs of other hungry people. But Jesus responded, "There's more to life than eating bread."

Our temptation for security takes other forms. We're tempted to get money so we can turn it not only into bread, but also clothes, cars, stereos, and records. But the temptation is the same: do what you have to do to assure your comfort and security.

If we think we are especially tempted to seek prestige and fame with our peers and others, look at Jesus' temptation (Matthew 4:5-7). Jesus had all the power of God at his disposal. What dazzling acts he could perform to draw attention to himself, to let the people know who he was. That temptation Jesus rejected too, for it would have been a misuse of power which he had as God's Son.

Again, this temptation is still with us today. However many good reasons there might be for being elected class president or being the football captain or having the highest grade point average in the student body, if these achievements become our goals in life, then we must examine our motives. Do we grasp for them because we want fame? Do we have something to prove to others? To ourselves?

If our temptation is to gain power over others, examine Jesus' temptation again (Matthew 4:8-10). Jesus could have attained any political goal he would set for himself. Yet he knew that to attempt to gain political power—to lord it over others, in other words—was really to turn control of his life over to Satan.

Although teenagers may seem to have little power, yet the temptation is there, is it not, to try to manipulate others (friends, family members, teachers) in subtle ways? We want to get them to do what we want.

We Can Withstand

Dietrich Bonhoeffer says that there are really only two temptation stories in the Bible. The first temptation was that of Adam's—that led to man's downfall. The second temptation was that of Christ's—that led to the downfall of Satan. Because Jesus was able to withstand temptation, we too can withstand; there is hope that we can overcome whatever temptations we face (Hebrews 4:15 and 2:17 f.).

This is partly a mystery. But why are we also able to withstand temptation?

For one thing, we have a positive example in Jesus. He reversed the example of the first man, Adam, who, when tempted, did not resist.

Second, in Jesus we find new purpose in life. No longer need we direct our attention inward upon ourselves. Our attention is directed outward toward Jesus, others, and God.

Finally, by the power of Jesus' resurrection and the presence of the Holy Spirit in the life of the Christian, victory is now possible. It is not assured, of course, since we still are human. But it is *possible*. And that makes all the difference.

A Prayer and a Song

We set ourselves up for temptation when:

• We travel with the crowd that likes to have beer bashes and pot parties;

• We spend long and passionate hours alone with our girlfriend or boyfriend;

• We become preoccupied with goals for earning money in our spare time and fantasies about how we'll spend it (on ourselves) once we've earned it.

The biblical response to evil is, flee from it. Run away from it, in other words. Don't test your endurance by seeing whether or not you can resist. Recognize your weakness.

When the Bible says we are to flee from evil (1 Corinthians 6:8; 10:14; 2 Timothy 2:22; 2 Peter 1:4), this doesn't mean to run away to some faraway and isolated place in the South Pacific. Wherever we are, we will still be

tempted to sin. We cannot get away from ourselves, our biggest tempter.

We can be assured of two things. That, one, we can, even when tempted, be delivered from sin. Jesus prayed to the Father that his disciples would not be led into temptation. Yet when they were, he asked that they not be delivered into evil; that is, that they not give in to sin.

And finally, when we do sin, we can be forgiven. We're not forgiven just so we can feel good for awhile and then go back and sin all over again. But we can truly be forgiven—that means to be restored to a right relationship with God and to righteous living.

If we confess our sins, he is
faithful and just, and will
forgive our sins and cleanse
us from all unrighteousness. (1 John 1:9)

Note the progression: we confess, then God forgives, and puts us back on the right track again (restores righteousness in our lives again).

This forgiveness, this cleansing, is not dependent upon any feelings we have at any particular time. It is dependent upon the grace of God in our lives. Even when we are feeling low about ourselves, we can trust God to forgive us and make us righteous. This should be our prayer: "Deliver us from evil." And this should be our song: "Thanks be to God, who in Christ always leads us in triumph, and through us spreads the fragrance of the knowledge of him everywhere" (2 Corinthians 2:14).

For Further Reading

Augsburger, Myron, *Walking in the Resurrection.*
    Scottdale: Herald Press, 1976.
Bonhoeffer, Dietrich, *Creation and Fall/Temptation.* 2
    volumes in one. New York: The Macmillan Press,
    1959/1953.

6. How Can I Cope with Personal Failure?

Most people have heard Murphy's Law: "If anything can go wrong, it will." Few people have heard O'Toole's response to Murphy's Law. He said, "Murphy was an optimist."

I don't know who O'Toole was. But he must have had not just one bad day, but a whole succession of bad days, when nothing would go right. Maybe he felt as though he wasn't just a failure at a few things but that his total life was a complete flop.

Is It Worth It?

We'll call her Sue. She was about 17 years of age, a student at a Christian high school, and a minister's daughter. When Sue came to me for help, she was in her senior year of high school and already felt as though her life had been a total failure. As a matter of fact, she didn't really feel that there was much to live for.

For one thing, she was overweight and didn't feel very attractive. She said she felt like a wallflower around her peers in school. No one noticed her, except when she made dumb mistakes, which she felt she was doing all the time.

Sue had a boyfriend, but instead of this relationship making her feel worthwhile, it only made her feel like a cheap plaything. There was nothing in the relationship beyond the level of making out. On top of this her boyfriend, who was older, wanted to get married as soon as she was out of school. Sue knew that their relationship was not a good one on which to build a meaningful marriage, yet she believed that it was her only chance to get married. So she felt trapped. She would marry someone she didn't really love or know very well.

Sue's relationships with her parents, at least from her point of view, were even worse. She could never tell her minister father or her mother her problems. In fact, Sue felt that her father was downright mean to her at home. Yet she was expected to put up a good front in church, since she was the minister's daughter. Her father had a reputation for being a very spiritual man. Sue thought he was a hypocrite. As for Sue's mother, she also seemed to be resentful toward her husband's dual life, but the mother took her resentment out on Sue, not on Sue's father.

Sue was young and had most of her life ahead of her, yet she believed herself to be a total failure. There was no future ahead of her, so she thought.

There are two different types of failure. In some cases of failure, there is hope for change. In a second kind of failure we cannot change the situation. In Sue's case there is hope for changing the status. True, Sue cannot suddenly become a "successful person" in life, but at seventeen there is time for her to discover her God-given abilities and begin to build a life on them.

But there are some situations in life that we cannot change. An older businessman in his mid-sixties can't suddenly make a change and become a professional musician. The die was cast long before. Perhaps he can take up music in retirement. But he can't go back and live life over.

Although we may not feel as clearly a failure as Sue, yet we all experience failure. It's not that we feel our life has been a complete waste; rather, we have experiences where we fall short of some ideal or standard. It may be either our own or someone else's. Why do we fail? How can we assure success? How can we cope with failure? What does it mean to succeed? These are some of the questions we will examine.

The Fear of Failure

Have you ever met a person who said, "I want to be a failure"? I haven't and suspect you haven't either. None of us wants to be a failure. Yet there is within us humans a strong sense of fear that we will fail.

When people were asked in a poll what their basic feeling is about life, 60 percent of the people responded with the word fear. There is much to be afraid of, especially in a nuclear age in which a few powerful people possess the capacity to end the world. However, much of our fear as humans is within us. We fear failure.

We do fail. To be human is to fail. Not every student can get straight A's, be elected president of the student council, or make the varsity basketball team.

And even those who make the team experience failure: turning the ball over too many times to the opposing team, missing a key shot in a close game, having to sit on the bench because there are many better players.

In learning how to cope with failure, we must be willing to recognize failure. The human mind likes to wipe out the unpleasant and remember only the good aspects of life. When we succeed, we say, "That's really the way I am. I'm a good student, or a good basketball player, or a good leader." But when we fail, then that is not the real us; we just had an off day. Or like the late Vince Lombardi, a football coach, once said, "We never really lost. We just ran out of time."

To recognize failure as failure means not just facing

up to it. It also means that sometimes we must realize that what we sense as failure is not really failure at all.

A part of being a teenager is learning what one can do and cannot do well. This is a part of the process of discovering who you are and who you might become. If you are in the process of discovering that you are not athletically inclined, perhaps you feel like a failure—as I did when I was in high school. But just because you cannot run at full speed and dribble a basketball at the same time doesn't mean you are a failure. You are only a failure at basketball and the world is much more than basketball.

All people have their own strengths and weaknesses. And no one notices these weaknesses better than you. You are the one who can't return a volleyball or sing on key. You feel that you stick out in a crowd when you can't do what everyone else seems to be capable of doing so easily. In reality, maybe no one else even notices, but you feel like a complete failure. You are your own worst critic, and that can cause you to feel like a failure. You would like to be admired.

Failure is not our inability to do something for which we haven't the gift or ability. Failure is not doing well in areas of life where we are well-gifted.

At the same time that we recognize our failure and our weaknesses, it is important to highlight our strengths. That will build up our self-confidence so that we don't become preoccupied with times when we do fall short of the goals we, or others, set for ourselves. We remember Babe Ruth as the baseball player who, until recent years, held the record for most home runs hit in a career. Who remembers that he also struck out 1330 times? If Babe Ruth would have allowed the 1330 strike-outs to get him down, he likely would not have hit 714 career home runs.

Failure can be helpful. Our failures can actually be learning experiences. E. W. Howe said, "Most of our problems are test questions." And what we learn from our mistakes may actually help us to avoid the same pitfalls in the future. For instance, a poor performance in school may be the result of being involved in too many activities. You may need to reexamine the use of your time.

In order to make something of ourselves, we have to be willing to risk failure. To play it safe by always choosing the easier of two options or setting small goals for ourselves may be the surest route to failure. It is to take the advice of Bob Hope, who told a college graduating class: "I'd like to offer a couple of words of advice to you young people about to go into the world. (Pause) Don't go."

Co-Creators with God

In an earlier chapter we said that we Christians are co-creators with God in planning the future. Together with God we are partners in shaping our destiny. We need not be frightened by this so that we can't act. Remember, we with God are co-creators of our future. God is our partner. He will be with us. His Spirit will guide us.

This does not mean we will always make the right decisions, or that we will always succeed and never fail. But when we do make mistakes, our divine partner waits for us, picks us up even, and then helps us resume our journey into the future.

When we fail we can experience the presence of God in our lives in a way unknown to us when we succeed. In failure we recognize our own weakness and our need for God. It is in our inadequacies that he can be most fully present with us. When we think we are strong we are likely not to recognize the need for God. God never forces himself on us; he comes to us as we are open to him. Unfortunately, too often we recognize our need for him only in failure.

Another source of strength for the Christian in lessening fear of failure is family. The Christian is a member of the family, the immediate family—your home—and the church family. At its best, a family will help make it possible for you to fail and also to succeed. A supportive family continues to treat you as an important son or daughter in spite of failures. Ultimately, in your family, your value is not judged by whether you are the top player on the hockey team or make it into the best college. Your value is that you are a son or daughter of the Unruh family or a member of the Diamond Avenue Brethren Church. This support in failure can also be your greatest help for success.

Another Kind of Failure, Another Kind of Success

Jesus told a story about a man who was highly successful. So successful was he at farming that his barns and silos and storage sheds couldn't hold all that he produced. What was he to do with all that he produced? What was he to do with all that he had grown?

Not content to put up merely an extra shed or two, the man tore down all the buildings he already possessed. And then he put up a completely new farm complex with all the latest equipment and with storage space to spare.

Then he seemed content with what he had. So he sat back, relaxed, and called in a few close friends for a party. They ate and drank and danced and had a grand time. But that night the good farmer passed away. All that he had accomplished was gone—at least as far as he was concerned.

Likely his friends said, "What a pity. He was just at the point in life where he could afford to feel secure. What a success he was turning out to be! If only he could have stayed around longer to enjoy it."

Jesus seems to say that if you're rich as far as earthly things are concerned, that doesn't mean you're rich as far as the things of God are concerned.

With God, all earthly notions of success are turned inside out. In fact, one writer calls God's kingdom *The Upside-Down Kingdom.* The signs of success for the world really count for nothing in God's sight.

Is it really a sign of success to be able to date the most popular girl or boy in school? Or to be the best football player on the varsity squad? Or to have the highest grade-point average in your class? Or to drive the neatest sports car at your school? Are these goals really worth striving for?

Before the Apostle Paul became a Christian, he had some of the best social credentials available to him as a Jew of his day. He was definitely with the "in" group—the popular, status-oriented people. Then when he became a Christian he gave that all up. What he had had before—social prestige, a sense of belonging—was nothing, he said, in comparison to what he found in Jesus Christ. All that he had in his former life was really garbage, as he called it (see Philippians 3:8). He was quite willing to give all that up for the peace, righteousness, and hope of eternal life he was discovering as a disciple of Jesus. Would you believe that he even claimed that to suffer is a small price to have to pay for identifying with Christ rather than with the world's standard of success?

The story of the Anabaptists is filled with people who suffered and were driven from one country to another in their attempt to follow Christ. They did not look for persecution but rather tried to live the new life of Jesus Christ. This often made them unpopular in militaristic societies. Their biographies would read like failures for those who believe success is found in might, wealth, and power to control. But we consider them to be faith heroes.

The Christian has a broader perspective. What the Christian has or doesn't have is set in an eternal framework. The things of the world will pass away. But the things of Christ will endure forever. Christians have a higher goal than power, prestige, wealth or earthly security. What we strive toward cannot be measured with human standards.

"Hold to Christ"

As a growing, maturing young person you are probably experiencing much change in your life. Not only are events in the world around us rapidly changing, but your own personal life is changing.

Perhaps you are encountering new ideas about the way the world is composed and how it functions. You may be deepening your understanding of how God works in this world. That is the purpose of this book. On top of all these changes you are shifting views of who you are and who you want to become.

During this change in life which can be dramatic, even shattering at times, the advice of Herbert Butterfield, a historian and a Christian, is helpful. His motto for life was: "Hold to Christ, and for the rest be totally uncommitted."

On the foundation of Christ, his teachings, his life, death, and resurrection, a purposeful and meaningful life can be built. Though everything else around us can come loose at the joints, this one thing will endure: Jesus Christ and his eternal kingdom. We might fail, but he will remain true.

For Further Reading

Augsburger, David, *Be All You Can Be.* Carol Stream, Illinois: Creation House, 1970.

Kraybill, Donald B., *The Upside-Down Kingdom.* Scottdale: Herald Press, 1978.

Thielicke, Helmut, *Being a Christian When the Chips Are Down,* Philadelphia: Fortress Press, 1979.